Top mentors and leaders share early praise for the latest book by
The Millionaire Mentor
Gregory Scott Reid

"Everyone needs a Mentor to get to the next level. The fast-moving book (***Positive Impact***) is an entertaining and helpful blueprint for you to follow."

Brian Tracy, Speaker and #1 Best-Selling Author
The 100 Absolutely Unbreakable Laws of Business Success

"Gregory Scott Reid is the new Zig Ziglar. I love this man. Just by reading a few chapters, I knew this book had to be an absolute mega bestseller. I admire his work and recommend it highly."

Steven E., Speaker and Creator of the #1 Best-Selling Series
Wake up…Live the Life You Love

"G.S.R. does it again. The author of *The Millionaire Mentor* shows us in Positive Impact the importance of supporting and depending upon each other to achieve and sustain success."

Harry Paul, #1 Best-Selling Co-Author,
Fish! And Fish! Tales

"The Millionaire Mentor's new book will force you to see how you can have anything in life you truly want. It will have an enormously Positive Impact on the way you look at your business and personal life."

John Assaraf, a.k.a. The Street Kid Speaker
#1 Best-Selling Author, *The Street Kid's Guide to Having It All*

"*Positive Impact* will mentor you into making millions. It is filled with wisdom and practical insights on how to run a company, boost moral, and improve results."

Ken D. Foster, CEO, Shared Vision Network
#1 Best-Selling Author, *Ask and You Will Succeed*

"Simple wisdom that's tremendously powerful. I dare you to read this book and not take away a few pearls that can immediately rock your world."

Bob Scheinfeld, Founder of The Ultimate Lifestyle Academy, #1 Best-Selling Author, *The 11th Element*

"Reid's new book will leave you with a POWER-FUL message while having a Positive Impact toward the way you think about running your business."

Mike Litman, #1 Best-Selling Co-Author
Conversations with Millionaires

"G.S.R. strikes gold again! Regardless of your previous levels of success, Positive Impact reveals insights that will take your business and personal lives to a whole new level. It is a must read for all of my employees and interns."

Richard M. Krawczyk, PhD (a.k.a.) Dr. Richard
#1 Best-Selling Author, *Financial Aerobics*

"Not since the One Minute Manager have I read as powerful a parable as Positive Impact. Mr. Reid has distilled volumes of text on team building and ethical business practices into an easy-to-read, informative, inspirational, and very motivating book. It's a must for all who want to better themselves and their team's productivity."

David M. Corbin, Speaker
Author, *Psyched on Service, Brandslaughter*

"This thought-provoking fable is a Masterpiece! America's favorite Mentor created a real gem that's easy-to-read and leaves you searching for ways to proactively make a difference in other people's lives."

Randy Gilbert,
Host of *TheInsideSuccessShow.com*

"Gregory Scott Reid's deceptively simple parable removes the complexity we create that prevents our own success. His high-touch business parable, *Positive Impact*, illustrates that the greatest way to find your success is by helping others find theirs first.

Martin Wales, The Customer Catcher™
Business Talk–Radio host,
www. Customer Catcher.com

"*Positive Impact* is inspiring and practical. Set in a delightful story, it illustrates what living with passion and purpose can do. Read it once—read it twice more. Be inspired and spread your inspiration. That is a life well lived. Bravo Greg!"

Mary Goulet, Radio Talk Show Host
Author of *MomsTown Guide to Getting a Life* (Hyperion Books 2005)

"The Millionaire Mentor has written a priceless story that teaches the business world how to attain enduring success by changing our views from focusing on profits, to focusing on people."

Joe Heaney,
Former President, CornNuts

POSITIVE
IMPACT

Also by GREGORY SCOTT REID

Author of the #1 best seller
The Millionaire Mentor
(Possibility Press)

Co-author of the #1 best seller
Wake up...Live the life you Love
(Little Seed Publishing)

Co-author of:
Walking with the Wise
(Mentors Publishing)

Co-author of:
Recovering your lost self from Adversity
(Personal Transformation Press)

Forward written for the #1 best seller
Financial Aerobics
(Cavalier Publishing)

POSITIVE IMPACT

Set Yourself on a Collision Course for Success

Gregory Scott Reid

LITTLE SEED PUBLISHING

Dedication

To all those who make a Positive Impact on others' lives—the mentors, parents, coaches, teachers, and dreamers.

In addition, special appreciation goes out to those who have supported me on this wonderful journey, while encouraging me along the way:

God

For with Him, all things are possible.

Steven E. • Lee Beard • Janet Althouse • David Corbin • Kay Torrans • Oscar Lopez • Rhonda Vowell • John Assaraf • Jeff Crolene • Jack DeLessio • Aunt Sandra • David Miller • Mary Gale Hinrichsen, PhD.

Thank you to all—"You have made a Positive Impact in my life, which will always be remembered."

Contents

Introduction

This book is a compilation of stories derived from my online newsletters. Each one was reconfigured to fit into this fable that describes real life events, which shaped my outlook on life and business success.

"The greatest success we'll know is helping others succeed and grow."

—Gregory Scott Reid

Treat Everyone Equally
— Equally Nice ❤

Chapter 1

Treat Everyone Equally

'MONDAY MORNINGS GET HERE way too fast,"
complains the thirty-five-year-old executive to
the woman behind the desk.

"You must be John Bishop. Mr. Cams will be with
you shortly," responds the neatly dressed lady,
motioning for the younger man to take a seat.

"Thank you," he says as he walks toward the sofa
and starts shuffling through his briefcase.

"I'm sorry we don't have any reading material.
Would you like to talk?" the woman asks kindly.

The young man doesn't know how to reply. He's
never heard a suggestion like that before, especially
from a "lowly" office receptionist. He sits, stunned,
like a deer caught in the headlights.

"Ummm, ahhh, that's okay. I have some papers to
review. Thanks anyway," he mutters as he continues
to go through his briefcase in obvious avoidance.

"Very well," the friendly woman says, smiling her
easy smile. "If there's anything you need, just ask. By

the way, what can I get you to drink? We have coffee, iced tea, soda, and water."

"Uhhh, nothing," the young man says, brushing her off once again. Annoyed and feeling even more uncomfortable than before, he thinks, Why the heck is this lady trying to talk to me? I mean, doesn't she know who I am?

John is one of those cocky people who think status is everything. To him, what people do for a living, where they live, which clubs they attend, and the size of their portfolios all indicate who they are as people. He snubs those he feels are insignificant and common. In his mind, a guy is only worth John's time if he's powerful, rich, successful, and able to help John get that way too.

That's why he's here today. He's read numerous articles about sixty-five-year-old Oscar Cams, the CEO of a major manufacturing company and the most respected entrepreneur in town. Everyone describes Cams as the epitome of success; everything he touches seems to turn to gold. John, feeling dissatisfied with his own career despite his quick rise to executive VP, wants to pick the older man's brain and learn the secrets to his success. Why does everyone rave about this guy? What makes him so special? How come he seems so happy and passionate about what he's doing, while I feel exactly the opposite? John wonders.

Interrupting his thoughts yet again, the woman behind the desk asks, "Do you have any pets, Mr. Bishop?"

"Look," he says condescendingly, "I'm here to meet with your boss, and I've been waiting over a month to get this appointment. Can't you just let me be for a while so I can prepare myself for this meeting?"

Then, before the polite woman can respond, an older, very fit, extremely energetic man pops his head out of an office door and says in a cheerful tone, "Hi! You must be John, the superstar vice president I've been hearing so much about. Come on into my office." Waving his arm toward the reception desk he adds, "By the way, did you get a moment to meet my wife, Ellen?"

Once again, John gets that frozen deer-in-the-headlights feeling, this time wishing someone would run over him and put him out of his misery.

"Yes, dear," she replies as John cringes at the irony of hearing her say, "Yes, deer."

"Fantastic! Then come on in here and let's get started," the successful businessman proposes.

A remorseful John walks through the solid oak doorway into Mr. Cams's office. He turns back to apologize, but Ellen raises her finger to her lips with an ever-so-silent "Shhhh" and winks at him. John realizes he's probably not the first to make such a bad impression. Gratefully, he smiles at her and mouths, "Thank you."

As young Mr. Bishop enters the room, he quickly forgets what just happened and his face lights up like a child in a toy store.

It seems as if he's walked back in time and stepped into an old movie house, complete with refurbished theater chairs against the wall and classic film posters hanging above them—Guys and Dolls, Casablanca, Singin' in the Rain. John is sure he smells the faint aroma of popcorn in the air. Mr. Cams's desk and chair sit in front of a giant window flanked on each side by red velvet draperies, resembling a cinema screen—but the screen is clear, shiny glass.

The view from the window reveals the inner workings of the host's factory, with a conglomeration of humming machinery and people zipping about. It reminds John of the ant farm that fascinated him as a child—two panels of glass with sand in between where he could watch ants at work firsthand.

"Wow!" exclaims John. "I know I'm supposed to be all composed when entering a business meeting, but I have to tell you, Mr. Cams—this place is exciting! My grandfather would have loved this!"

"Who was your grandfather?" asks Mr. Cams in the politest of ways.

"Jacob Bishop. He used to run—" begins John, but the older gentleman pipes in and finishes his words.

"The Three Palm Theater down on Market Street," shouts Mr. Cams in obvious excitement. "He was a GREAT man! One of our first customers, in fact. What ever happened to that old theater, anyway? That place was fantastic."

"My dad inherited it when my grandfather passed away," John replies. "Dad promised to rebuild it one day, but that day never came and now it just sits empty. I always hoped to reopen it one day in my grandfather's honor."

"Now, that's a great idea," replies the older gentleman. "Have a seat and let's hear what else is on your mind."

As the guest sits, he can't keep his eyes off the window and all the action.

"I suppose it's difficult for new visitors to stay focused with such a show before them," John observes.

"It's funny you use that word show to describe my family here," Mr. Cams replies.

"Family?" asks John.

"Yes, but before we cross that bridge, let me ask you why you've been working so hard to meet with me. I have to tell you, I appreciate your moxie, young man. Your persistence was quite impressive and I've heard good things about you. So, share with me, what can I do for you?"

"Well, it's like this," begins the visitor. "As you may have heard, I've done pretty well these past few years, becoming a VP with my company and all. However, I feel as though I'm capped out, like I hit a self-imposed glass ceiling of sorts, and I can't progress. I was wondering—well, hoping really—if you could help me figure out what I'm doing wrong."

"You seem like a bright young man, John, and I seriously doubt that you don't know exactly what you're doing wrong." The student just sits there dumbfounded as the older man continues, "I'm sure I can show you a few more things you could be doing right, though."

"I don't get it. What's the difference?" asks John with genuine interest.

"It's like this," says Mr. Cams. "You've achieved a high level of success. You've done that by making a great number of good decisions, but none of us make good decisions all the time.

"Let me ask you this, John—do you like what you're doing? Do you have a real passion for it? I'm willing to bet the answer is no."

"How did you know?" asks the young entrepreneur.

"Because I was just like you," admits the mentor. "I thought I knew everything when I was your age, but the one thing I didn't know was what I wanted to do with my life. I had great success in most things I did, but no real excitement for them."

The younger man grins and nods. "That's exactly where I am, Mr. Cams," he replies.

"So, to tell you the things you're doing wrong would be a waste of time and energy for both of us. What I can offer you, instead, are some ideas of what more you could do right and a glimpse into our family here. By sharing with you my passion, perhaps I can shine some light on a few ideas you can apply to your business. In the process, you might find your passion like I did."

"Sounds great," beams the eager student.

"But before we begin, you have to promise me one thing in regard to what I share with you."

"To keep it a secret between us, I bet," John says quickly.

"No! Heavens no," Mr. Cams laughs. "The complete opposite is what I want you to promise me. Everything I share with you, you must share with at least one other person."

The young entrepreneur just sits in silence, the expression on his face similar to that of Mr. Spock in a Star Trek episode—one eyebrow quizzically higher than the other.

"*Wellll, okaaay,*" John agrees, sounding a little befuddled.

"Great!" booms his mentor. "Come back in the morning at 0700 hours. We'll go from there. Be sure to lose that tie and wear comfortable shoes. We're a hands-on environment here."

"Outstanding," acknowledges the pupil, and he reaches out to Mr. Cams to shake his hand in appreciation.

"Nonsense," replies Mr. Cams as he walks around his desk and gives John a good old-fashioned bear hug.

The startled newcomer stands there for just a moment, waiting to see if what he thought just happened really had.

Then, as John turns to leave, Mr. Cams asks, "By the way, young man, did you learn one of the first new things to do right today?"

The young man faces his adviser, looks curious, and admits, "I must have missed it. What was it?"

"It is right outside that door. I always keep the intercom on before I meet with someone new so I can hear how they treat people other than me. If you'd known the woman at the reception desk was my wife, you probably would have been more cordial, don't you think?"

The young man's face turns red as he regretfully admits, "Yes—yes, I would have."

"Well, there you go," Mr. Cams responds. "Look at the banner hanging above the doorway to my office, John. I think maybe you missed that, too."

Following the older man's instructions, John sticks his head out the door, looks up, and reads the banner hanging there:

MR. CAMS CONTINUES, "The first thing to do right is to treat everyone equally—equally nice—because you don't know who the person next to you at a ballgame, in an elevator, driving alongside your car, or even sitting at the reception desk of a large corporation might be. Would you like to learn a way to treat everyone equally nice?"

"I'm all ears," says John.

"The most important thing you can do is take time to talk to people," reveals Mr. Cams, "just like I'm doing here with you today. Instead of being totally absorbed in yourself and your busy life, take time to look up and talk to the people you come in contact with each day. Don't just fly by with a quick hello. Stop and talk. You can learn a lot from talking to people. Do you have time for a quick story, John?"

"You bet!" the student says, now quite fascinated by his mentor's approach, and pleased that Mr. Cams is spending so much time with him.

"A man I know, who goes by the initials G.R., started a company in a little business park—a low-budget kind of place for upstarts. Across the hall from him was a group of older gentlemen who ran an organization called the Distinguished Flying Cross Society.

"Well, after months went by with G.R. just glancing a friendly hello their way, bumping into the guys in the hallway and whatnot, he finally went over to see what these fellows were all about.

"Knocking at the door, he found their leader, a man named Jack, kneeling on the floor and shuffling some papers. Wearing one of those tweed jackets with leather patches on the elbows, Jack looked like a former college professor.

"As G.R. leaned inside the doorway just outside the office, he discovered that those older gentlemen were a hoot. They were pilots who'd flown in combat and survived to tell their stories. Each had received the Distinguished Flying Cross, an Armed Forces medal awarded for heroism or extraordinary achievement. They were heroes in every sense of the word, and they'd started their society to publicize the meaning of the award and to honor its recipients. In addition, they established scholarships, arranged reunions, conducted tours, and much more.

"As they spoke, G.R. couldn't help but wonder about Jack. He said, 'I have to tell you, this organization you run is absolutely the best. What's your background? How do you hold everything together so well? I mean, did you manage a business, teach business courses, or do something like that before doing this?'

"Jack, without blinking, looked up at his visitor standing there in the doorway and responded, 'You could say that.'

"'Well, what was it? Did you manage or teach?' G.R. pressed further.

"'I ran a company,' Jack said with pride.

"'Was it a big company? Were you the GM, VP, or what?' G.R. continued.

"In an authoritative voice, Jack replied, 'I'd say it was a company that started small, with a big idea, and turned into a large corporation after many years of trial and error.' Still shuffling through the scattered papers, Jack continued, 'The title I held was one of many. You see, son, when you're immersed in your passion, doing what you love and believe in, the words beneath your name on your stationery don't really matter. What we're doing here right now at this moment is what means the most, not the title that goes with it. But, with that said, in the business world I suppose I was considered the CEO.'

"G.R. stood there for a moment. He'd been preparing to hand his gold-leafed business card—with his title larger than his name—to this man. Instead, he put it back in his pocket. With his head lowered and his ego in check, he let out a deep sigh. He was feeling silly.

"Snickering softly, feeling a little deflated, but open to learning more, he said, 'I think I need to go burn my business cards. Then I'd like to take you out to lunch someday soon so you can hand down more of your words of wisdom to me. I'm new at this game, and I'd greatly appreciate any input you're willing to pass along. Can we do that sometime soon?'

"'Sure, let's shoot for tomorrow,' said Jack. "G.R. beamed. 'Great!' he said. As he turned to leave Jack's patriotically decorated red-white-and-blue office, the rookie stammered out this fateful question to his new friend, 'By the way, what was the name of the company you ran, Jack?'

"Still shuffling through the papers on his floor, Jack quickly looked up and asked, 'Have you ever heard of Velcro?'"

"Wow! What a great story and lesson. Thank you, Mr. Cams," says John.

"And one day," continues Mr. Cams, "you may be that person passing along your words of wisdom."

With that, the first meeting comes to an end. John has already learned decidedly more than he expected. He thought he knew everything but feels differently now and can't wait for tomorrow.

Chapter 2

We ARE the Company We Keep

"GOOD MORNING, MRS. CAMS," says our young friend John as he walks into the office with a completely different attitude than the day before.

"Hello, Mr. Bishop. May I get you something?" the sharply dressed Mrs. Cams offers in the friendliest tone.

"No, thank you. I want to say I'm sorry about the way I acted yesterday and . . ."

Before John can finish his apology, Mr. Cams plows through the room like a freight train off its tracks. "Come along, boy. We've got things to do," he says as he steams full force across the reception area floor, straight through his office door.

"You'd better get going, young man," Mrs. Cams urges, "or you'll never catch up."

Noticing John's startled look of Which way did he go? she shouts, "Run!" while pointing toward the direction of Mr. Cams's exit.

Young John, not used to such excitement this early in the morning, finally catches up with his leader, who is bent down at a trash receptacle picking up candy wrappers that hadn't made it into the can.

John races to his side and blurts out, "Why are you doing this? Shouldn't the janitor or someone else clean this up?"

Mr. Cams drops the wrappers into the bin, stands up straight, and says, "Here's a quiz for you, John. Say you have some very important business associates coming to your office one morning and the cleaning staff didn't make it in the night before. Now the bathrooms and everything else are a mess, but you want to make a good impression. Do you (a) call the cleaning crew and chew them out, (b) leave it— because it's not your job, or (c) clean it yourself?"

John stands there frozen. Once again, the protégé is surprised and a little embarrassed by Mr. Cams's savvy yet humble demeanor. "Well," begins John, feeling a little like he's in elementary school again, "since I'm the vice president of the corporation, I probably would ask someone else to come in and do it."

"John, that's a shame," sighs Mr. Cams, shaking his head in disappointment. "You'll never be a leader with that kind of thinking."

"Why? What are you talking about? I already am a leader. Remember my company? I'm the senior executive VP of a very successful advertising firm."

"Just because you have a title and pay people to do what you say, doesn't make you a leader. You can't be a leader if no one follows you," reprimands his coach.

"Real leaders do whatever it takes, whenever needed, without question or hesitation, while taking into account the best interest of all those around them. The best leaders are those who are humble and act as they did when they were attempting to secure their position, even though they already have the position. A title and money won't gain you respect. Respect must be earned."

John stands in silence as Mr. Cams continues, "Right here, right now, I would graciously roll up my sleeves and help empty the trash, make the coffee, train the new guy—whatever task needs to be done. True leaders can work side by side with their staff or do it alone. And, do you know what? Since my family here knows I feel this way, guess how many times they've had to request any sort of chores from me?"

"Never, I suppose," replies the slightly deflated student.

"Finally you're right about something," teases the mentor. "But I'm sure you're missing the final piece of this message. You see, they wouldn't have to ask me, because they know that I, or anyone else in our company, would gladly volunteer to help out—without being asked—because we're family."

"Wow, I don't know what to say," surrenders the guest. And before John can say anything else, Mr. Cams launches into the following story.

"I remember coming into the office to work late one night and finding my janitor's son, Charlie, cleaning. When I asked why he was here instead of his father, he said that his dad was sick with the flu and couldn't make it in. Rather than let the family down, his father had sent him. Well, actually, the young man had volunteered to do it, because he knew how much his father appreciated his job, and he felt it was the right thing to do.

"You know what? That kid and I stayed here all through the night scrubbing this place from top to bottom, just as his Pop, as he called him, would have done. I swore Charlie to secrecy so no one would know it was us who did the work.

"That was two years ago, and Charlie is now my shipping department manager. His father has retired, never having to work again because, due to his loyalty, he is and always will be treated like one of the family. Do you get the picture now, John?"

"I think so," says John. "The son was taken on board because he'd already earned your respect and proven himself through his actions. I mean, who wouldn't want someone like that working in their company?"

"Exactly! You can't buy that kind of loyalty, John. Either you have it or you don't, and those who have it are the only ones I choose to surround myself with. That's why I don't hesitate to clean up a few scraps of paper around a trash can, because it will help the new janitor who is, again, my family. For gosh sakes, haven't you ever helped your mother clear the dinner table?"

"Okay, okay, I get it," says the student in an accepting tone. "But why do you call everyone here family?"

"Great question! I was wondering how long it would take for you to bring that up again," Mr. Cams congratulates John as though he just picked the winning lottery numbers.

"Let me begin by telling you that my wife and I didn't start this company, dear boy. My father, who inherited it from his father, handed it down to me. Each of us improved the company and created new concepts under our tenures. The rule has always been: Find your passion, and then use the company as a vehicle to achieve it. So now, even though our company has changed over time, we still are and always will be a family-run organization. And I want to keep it that way."

"But now you get to choose your family," quips the pupil, attempting a little humor. "Boy, it would be nice if you could choose all of your family members. I know for sure that everyone in my family would choose to enjoy Thanksgiving dinner without my tipsy Uncle Paul."

The two chuckle a bit at John's quick wit. "Even though we can't choose our family, we can choose who we associate with," continues the wise Mr. Cams. "You see, young man, I believe we are exactly where we have chosen to be, because our circumstances, accomplishments, and even our setbacks are a direct result of the actions we choose. You put yourself here today, John, because of the actions you took to get to meet me. Have you learned anything yet?"

"Yes," says John. "In fact, I need a bigger notebook and more pens."

Mr. Cams smiles and recounts, "Someone once said we are an accumulation of the five people we associate with most—and our income is the average of those same five people as well.

"It's like when you were in high school. If you hung around with the kids who smoked, who were you?"

"A smoker, I suppose," mutters the guest.

"And if you hung around with the athletes, the math whizzes, or the chess club people?"

"The same would apply there as well. You'd probably be like the others in the group you associated with," says John, reflecting on the comment he's just made.

"So," Mr. Cams continues, "I did some serious soul searching on that notion, and it came to me like a bolt of lightning: From this day forward, I will choose the company I keep. At that moment, Mrs. Cams and I began our quest to surround ourselves with people who share our values. Let's see—now where did I see that?" asks Mr. Cams jokingly as he stands beneath another banner adorning the hallway, his eyes rolling upward in its direction.

"INTERESTING," replies young John.

"Now, here's the best part," says Mr. Cams. "Once we started surrounding ourselves with the best people, with the best intentions, we started receiving the best in return, for water seeks its own level. We chose to raise that level and—voilà—created our own family environment with like-thinking members."

"I see," says John. "But how can you be sure that everyone is like-thinking and shares your same level of enthusiasm about things? They may end up raining on your parade, so to speak."

"Absolutely that could happen," says Mr. Cams. "Unfortunately, I don't have a banner on this one," he replies with a grin. "But I like to refer to this as anchors away."

"Anchors away?" questions John.

"Many years back, I noticed more and more people talking about 'clearing out the closet' and taking personal inventory of the people they associate with most.

"One of my favorite quotes is 'Avoid the ugly people.' Now, this has nothing to do with physical appearance, mind you; it's a comment to illustrate that to really achieve our goals and wants, we should surround ourselves with other like-minded people to support us on our journey. To make that quantum leap toward personal happiness and success in our lives, sometimes we just need to clean house of our own 'ugly people' who for some strange reason we feel the need to hold onto."

"I can relate to that incredibly well," says John in a somber tone. "I had a business associate in my past who went along with me on every job. He constantly told me that it was due to his so-called guidance that I found all my success, and that he kept me grounded so I stayed on course and progressed in the right direction. He used to call himself the anchor of our relationship, for without him, he would say, I'd go off and mess things up by chasing all my wild ideas and acting on concepts that weren't time tested."

"Did this bother you?" asks the older man.

"Well, to be honest, at first—no, it didn't. I actually believed then that if I listened to what he told me and avoided all the horrors of going forward with my plans, it would save me years of heartache. Because, again, I thought of him as my anchor, as you said."

"I think you just gave me a better example than I was going to share with you," laughs Mr. Cams. "Let me see if I can finish your story. The person in fact was your anchor—he was weighing you down and holding you back! He was the anchor that kept you from smiling forward toward living the life you love by chasing your dreams and sharing your ideals for success. Considering that you referred to him as someone from the past, you've obviously already learned the meaning of letting go, or in other words . . . anchors away!"

Young John stands there in deep reflection while nodding in agreement and whispering to himself, "It's so simple."

"Now, with that said," continues Mr. Cams, "you can see why it's so important that even though our company has grown to accommodate hundreds of people, each person is like-thinking. They're chosen by us or referred to us by one of our own, because we all understand that our mission is to help everyone succeed together and not hold anyone back. We care about each other like family. If someone's out sick, it's not uncommon for someone else to work extra hours to do their work. If someone needs help sending their kids to college, we have a program to assist them with that. And if—"

"Someone sees a piece of paper on the floor, they pick it up to help someone else out," John interrupts, finishing his mentor's sentence.

Mr. Cams pauses again, smiles brightly, and gives his pupil a wink of agreement. "You know something, young man? At this rate you may just 'get it' after all. And we haven't even made it past the trash can yet!"

John smiles back as Mr. Cams whispers these words, "Psssst—here's the secret. You know how they say to treat people like you want to be treated?"

"Yes," replies John.

"It's a lie," says the mentor.

John stands there puzzled once more, wondering what's coming next.

"Treat people the way they want to be treated," says John's adviser, in the warmest of tones. "You see, we all have different ideas, dreams, and desires. Find out what those things are for each person and talk to them about their interests," Mr. Cams says as he throws his arm around his newest friend's shoulders.

Turning John toward the door that leads into the factory, the mentor whispers these final words into John's ear, "The more you know about people, the easier it is to treat them as they want to be treated. You'll also create friends and alliances, and you'll gain respect. Now, let's go meet the family."

Chapter 3

Be a Star!

A S THE TWO MEN PUSH through the large
swinging doors leading into the factory, John
can't help but notice the giant banner hanging
from the rafters. It reads:

The younger man's attention is drawn to the people bustling all around, yet none of the machinery is moving. It appears they're getting ready to close down the shop for an extended time—preparing for a long vacation or something.

"What's going on?" inquires John.

"Spring cleaning," answers Mr. Cams. "I'm glad you came today to see how we keep things new within these old walls."

"You've got that right," agrees John. "This place looks excellent. I've never seen a factory so clean and well organized before. What's the secret?"

Mr. Cams leads the way to an area perched above the factory floor and begins to explain. Pointing down toward the middle of the work area, he says, "Well, it's simple, really—not rocket science or some crazy new idea—and we're so used to it, we hardly think about it anymore."

"So, what is it?" the young entrepreneur asks eagerly.

"We switch," replies the mentor.

"Switch?" inquires John.

"You see, every six months to a year, we switch our general labor positions. That way we get our family cross-trained in every job here," explains Mr. Cams.

"Doesn't that scare the employees? Aren't they afraid they may lose their job security?"

"Well, let me ask you. Who would be more valuable at your company, young man, someone who knows how to do one thing, or someone who knows how to do everything? I compare it to having a paring knife or a Swiss Army knife—one with all the bells and whistles. If you were out in the woods, which one would have more value?"

Even though the look on the young man's face shows his agreement, his head fills with a frightening vision of the mass hysteria such a bold move would cause within his corporation.

"Now, I know what you're thinking," says Mr. Cams, "and to be honest, I thought the same thing when someone first suggested this idea to me many years ago. You think people are going to jump ship, right?"

John nods yes, with a look on his face that says, How did he know what I was thinking?

The older gentleman continues, "To be honest, a few of our employees did jump ship when we first started this switching thing. But it's become such a habit now, as I said, that no one thinks twice about it anymore. As for the newer employees, this is all they know. And to be honest, we all now look forward to switching day.

"Have you ever had a job that you wished you could have switched with someone else in the company? Well, this is their opportunity to do just that.

The best thing, believe it or not, is that each new person adds his or her own twist to the fresh assignment. By the simple laws of evolution, the position eventually streamlines itself. The way a job is done now—let alone a year ago or five years ago—is more productive and efficient than ever before."

"Who suggested this to you?" inquires John. "A vice president? An auditing firm?"

"You'd think so, but actually it came from one of our three-star suggestions," replies the teacher.

"Three-star what?"

"Let me explain, John. You see, on our company's anniversary, during our annual potluck dinner, each employee can submit three suggestions that he or she feels would improve the company. The suggestions can pertain to any of the departments because, after all, we 'switch' departments. Then we implement the best ideas. If we use an idea of yours, for example, you receive a thousand dollars in cash; a plaque is presented to you in front of all of your peers; and your name is engraved on the Walk of Fame. Do you see the Walk of Fame down there?"

Mr. Cams points to the floor leading into what appears to be the lunchroom. John notices that the entire area is decorated in the same movie theater style he saw in his mentor's office, with stars on the ground like the ones in Hollywood. Each star is inscribed with an employee's name.

"Holy smokes! That's a great idea," exclaims John. "They must love it."

"Yes, we all do," agrees Mr. Cams, "and it stays consistent with our movie motif theme."

"So, what you have here," says John, "is a company full of cross-trained, happy, motivated, family-oriented people all working together to create success."

"That's right, and we have fun doing it, too," replies the mentor. "I picked up a great little book a while back that you've probably heard of. It's called Fish!—A Remarkable Way to Boost Morale and Improve Results, and it was co-authored by Stephen C. Lundin and a friend of mine, Harry Paul. It's an amazing story of how these guys took a smelly job like selling fish at Pike Place Market in Seattle and turned it into a world-famous tourist attraction."

"How so?" asks John with sincere interest.

"They took what most would view as a horrible work environment and turned it into one of the most enjoyable, positive, and energetic places to work in America. They made the best of their conditions by having fun with them. They throw the fish across the room, behind their backs, and over their customers' heads, and they even make them talk with their hands inside like puppets. At the end of the day, they sell huge amounts of product while having the time of their lives. And people come from across the globe to watch these guys at work.

"The moral of the story, I thought to myself, is that if these guys could make the most of what they had to work with, just imagine what insurance agencies, real estate offices, accounting firms, and all other businesses could do."

"It reminds me of that old saying: When you love your work, you'll never work a day in your life. John asks, "How did you use this concept for your place?"

"We made work fun, just like you've seen, by creating the movie theater theme and the Walk of Fame, and establishing ongoing contests," replies the mentor.

"Contests?"

"Yep. One of the best parts of working here is the new contests we're always running. The employees come up with fun, innovative ways to help increase morale and revenue at the same time. Last month we held a Lobster Feast."

"Say what?" asks John.

"We hung plastic lobsters and other sea doodads we found at a party supply store all over the place— from the ceilings, the walls, the doors—wherever!

Then, when production went up by our projected goal of 12 percent (which had never been done before, by the way), we had a lobster feast. We flew in a boatload of live Maine lobsters and cooked them up right out in the parking lot. The family pitched in and set up tables and chairs outside, and arranged for the rest of the fixins', and before you knew it, we were having a crustacean extravaganza!

"From that big push by our team, revenues increased and profits more than covered the cost of the feast. And we're on track to do it again this month, because now everyone knows it's possible— the momentum is there for ongoing profit."

"That's just incredible. I don't know what to say," exclaims John. Then he asks his next question with sincere interest, "Do all of the contests include an expensive payout?"

"Absolutely not," assures the mentor. "In fact, one of the best ones we ever did, and had a blast doing, was called Boss for the Day. It didn't cost a dime."

"What did you do?" asks the engaged student.

"For one full week, in each department, whoever produced the highest volume with the fewest errors got to be Boss for the Day the following Monday.

"Whoever won in their division would show up at the factory (if they chose to) in a suit or nice outfit instead of their work smock, sit in the boss's office, enjoy a cup of coffee, and act as the manager for the entire day—while the supervisor worked the winner's position in return. It was great! Now we're doing it all the time," brags the proud adviser, "because we began to see that some employees can rise up to take on a managerial role, and it keeps the supervisor in touch with the staff at the same time."

"Talk about a freebie win-win proposition," exclaims the young Mr. Bishop.

The mentor smiles and winks at his impressed protégé, puts his arm around John's shoulders, and begins leading him down a flight of stairs toward the middle of the workplace.

"Let me introduce you to somebody," announces Mr. Cams. "Maria, come over here for a second, won't you, please? John, this is my right-hand woman, Maria, or as we call her around here, the director," says Mr. Cams as he introduces his manager to the young guest.

"Hello. Nice to meet you," smiles John as he reaches out and shakes Maria's hand. "Mr. Cams has been so kind to show me around your impressive organization and teach me some of your secrets."

Smiling warmly at the introduction, Maria replies, "It's great to meet you as well. However, what you're learning is no secret. We want everyone to share this information and succeed in his or her own company. Let me ask you, do you think you could implement some of these ideas in your company?"

"Well," John ponders, "it's not that I think people would reject the ideas as much as I think that . . ."

"So you don't think people will be receptive, do you?" interrupts Mr. Cams.

"That's not what I said," John protests.

"That's exactly what you said, young man," lectures the mentor as Maria continues the message.

"You see, John, one of the things Mr. Cams teaches us is to listen to what people are telling us, rather than what they're saying."

John tilts his head to one side, like a puppy about to learn a new trick.

"It's like this," Maria continues. "After watching and studying human behavior, Mr. Cams has noticed a few trends that changed the way we all look at and listen to others. He refers to them as his 99 percent rules. It's probably even closer to 100 percent, but our mentor here gives himself a little 'out' for those of us who want to find a loophole in his theory. We haven't found many loopholes, but we have discovered that looking for these common denominators in everyday conversation helps us to read between the lines more quickly.

"After years of studying human interaction, Mr.

Cams came up with a few 99 percent rules that really seem to work. First, when someone starts a sentence with 'It's not,' he's usually trying to tell you 'It is,' without hurting your feelings. Second, when someone starts a sentence with 'I don't,' she's trying to tell you 'I do.'

"Here are some examples," Maria continues. "If a person says, 'It's not you, it's me,' he's struggling to tell you, 'It's you.' When he says, 'It's not that you're too short,' he's actually thinking you are too short. Someone might say, 'It's not that I have a drinking problem,' but then goes on to tell a story about a time he drank too much. Get the picture?"

John nods yes, the wheels of his mind spinning rapidly.

"You see, John," adds Mr. Cams, "when I interrupted you a minute ago, it was because you said, 'It's not that I think people would reject the idea.' Using my 99 percent rule, I knew you were telling me that you thought people would reject the idea."

"Here's how I use the 99 percent rule every day," continues Maria, "to help me cut to the chase and find out what's really on someone's mind.

"For example, let's say that a salesperson comes into my office and begins a pitch with, 'It's not that we need the money, we're simply trying to help you gain a new product line for your corporation.' Now, whatever comes out of this person's mouth next doesn't really make a difference, because I know by using this rule that what he really wants is to raise capital. So I would stop him mid-sentence and say, 'Listen, you need money and I could use your product. Forget the five dollars that you want for each unit. Let me save us both some time. I'll give you what you really want—cash! I can give you two dollars each. Do you want it?'

"You see, once you master listening to what people are actually telling you, it puts you in control and can save a lot of time and hassle in the long run," Maria concludes.

"I get it," nods the younger man. "Now, what was the other rule you were talking about?" he asks eagerly.

Maria continues, "The other example I mentioned was the phrase, 'I don't,' as in 'I don't want to tell you.' When someone starts a sentence with 'I don't want to tell you,' she's usually trying to direct you without hurting your feelings. For example, 'I don't want to tell you how to raise your children, but—' or, 'I don't want to tell you how to drive, but—' or, 'I don't want to tell you to take my side, but—'"

"That's great!" blurts out the young Mr. Bishop. "Absolutely great! I hear those words every day. It's kind of like the word try in my office."

The manager and her boss look at John, puzzled. "Please continue," Mr. Cams urges.

"You kept using the word try in your examples. They try not to hurt your feelings. As we all know, try means to fail or simply not do something. When you ask someone, 'Hey, are you going to the party tonight?' and they respond, 'I'll try,' that pretty much means no, right? So when I need something done around my office, I listen for that word and then run from it."

Maria and Mr. Cams chuckle a bit, nodding in agreement as John continues his thought.

"It's like this. When I go up to someone and ask, 'Can you get this report on my desk by 9 A.M. tomorrow?' and they say, 'I'll try,' I simply take the document back from them and ask someone else. If they, too, say they'll try to get it done, I continue on my quest until I run into that one person who says, 'No problem.' That's the person who gets the job."

"Excellent!" says Mr. Cams. "I think you've got it! It's like when someone says it's the last thing he wants to do, it usually becomes the first thing he actually does. Like when a person says, 'The last thing I want to do is hurt your feelings, but I'm breaking up with you,' or 'The last thing I want to do is tell you how to do your job.'"

"But—" say John and Maria in unison.

Laughing, Mr. Cams says, "Well, I think we've all learned a little something new today. John, why don't you roam around on your own for a bit, and then join us for lunch in an hour in the theater?"

"Theater? Sounds great," says John. "I'll see you there. It's not that I'll be hungry by then."

Grinning at John's play on words, Mr. Cams and Maria leave their guest to explore on his own.

Chapter 4

Mentoring Your Way to Million$

"THIS PLACE IS GREAT!" booms John as he walks into the lunchroom with a tone and stride like he owns the place.

"Glad you think so," responds Maria. Then, noticing the three smiling faces at his side, she adds, "It looks like you found some new friends."

"Sure did," says John. "This is Marcos, Sharon, and Hank."

"Yes, I know—they're family," responds Maria.

"That's why they look familiar," teases Mr. Cams.

John grins sheepishly as his cheeks redden. "I feel like I've known these people for years," he says. "Great people and a great environment. This place is dynamite. I've learned more about high-quality manufacturing in this last hour than in my previous ten years."

"What new thing did you learn?" asks Sharon as she turns to face John.

"Well, I learned, first and foremost, that there are no such things as secrets."

The whole group cringes a bit and stares at him with a look of wonder.

"Let me explain," John continues. "For years, I thought many of the things I was doing were my original thoughts and ideas. I swore everyone to secrecy about my great 'trade secrets' to success and even kept many thoughts to myself so no one would steal them. Then I take a quick walk through your plant and find that not only are my so-called secrets not so secret, but everyone here is doing them better than me."

Mr. Cams and his family laugh.

"Everyone I talked to today shared their thoughts with me openly. Each one knows what the other one is doing. And they all help one another; notice I didn't say—try to help one another. I'm definitely impressed. I've never seen a company operate so smoothly. Like I said, this place is dynamite."

"You make a good point," says Marcos. "I never thought about it before, because this is the only way I know. I was hired right out of school; this was my first job, and the only job I've ever had. I thought every company ran this way. I mean, why would you keep secrets and keep your own people in the dark?"

The group turns quickly to John with looks on their faces that seem to say, Yeah, why would you have secrets?

John begins to chuckle and says, "I bet every organization in the world thinks they have the greatest ideas and no one else knows them. While the administration department keeps sales in the dark, the sales staff hides stuff from accounting, and the shipping department is the last to know anything. The only person who knows everything is the receptionist at the front desk. Meanwhile, some little shop in Kansas is probably doing the exact same thing, only more efficiently and never knowing it's some 'great wisdom' somewhere else."

The lights in the lunchroom suddenly grow dim. Mr. Cams turns to John and whispers, "Well, it looks like it's show time. Let's move along while the family enjoys their break. I want to show you something."

As people begin scrambling for seats, a large screen drops down from the ceiling, and a familiar face pops up and begins speaking.

"Isn't that Zig Ziglar, the author and motivational speaker?" asks John as he and Mr. Cams exit the theater toward their next quest.

"Sure is," replies the mentor. "Once a week, we

play inspirational messages on the big screen for the family. The other days, they usually watch TV or play games during their break."

"Unbelievable," John whispers, shaking his head.

"What's so unbelievable about that?" inquires his mentor.

"What if they get so inspired that they leave and open their own company?" he asks.

"That would be great," says Mr. Cams.

"What?" shrieks John.

"I said, that would be great," repeats the adviser. "Let me give you an example. I call it mentoring your way to millions. It's a powerful message and, in today's business environment, I believe it's time to dust it off and share it with others once more.

"You've heard it time and time again from our man Zig: To get what you want out of life, you must first help others get what they want. Reacquainting your-self with this principle is not only a good way to live, it's a great way to do business.

"Over the years, I've watched many start-up com-panies come and go. Their failures and setbacks got me wondering what happened. Where did they go wrong? But then I began to ask a bigger question, rephrased in a more positive manner—What did all the successful businesses do right? The answer is right there in the first thing I said, summarized like this:

"The more you mentor others, share what you know, learn, and earn, the more you solidify your chances to succeed at any endeavor. Commit to mentoring, and you can literally mentor your way to millions!

"Say you run a business—large or small. If it's your true desire to help everyone succeed, from the receptionist to the CEO (yourself), guess what? You will. Just help others get what they want first, and your own success will soon follow.

"Okay, right now you're asking yourself, 'How can I do that?'"

"You've got that right," John agrees in a curious tone.

"It's simple, really. The first thing you need to do is find out what motivates the people around you and commit to helping them achieve it. The second thing is to know who really counts in the company. Over the years, if there's one thing I've learned, it's that two of the most important positions in any organization are receptionists and sales executives."

"Why?" asks John.

"They're the people who interact most with your customers, and they're the people with the greatest potential to create new customers," continues Mr. Cams. "Happy receptionists and loyal, motivated sales reps are ambassadors for your company's positive image.

"Let's take that receptionist you were talking about earlier to illustrate how easily mentoring your way to millions can work—and work it does!

"Let's say your receptionist wants to go back to school to study nursing. We'll call her Nancy—we won't use my wife for this example, because you'd probably just be rude to her," teases Mr. Cams as John cringes. "Nancy tells you about this goal during the one-on-one orientation meeting you have with every new staff member, the meeting where you ask, 'If you could choose any career for yourself, what would you choose?'

"Once she's shared her goal with you, you congratulate her on a great choice of career paths and tell her you're going to help make her dream a reality. Now, Nancy is no fool. Of course not—you don't hire fools because 'We are the company we keep.' Remember?"

John smiles and nods yes.

"She may even ask why you'd support her in something that will eventually cause her to leave your organization—just as you're wondering right now. You tell her, 'Nancy, you are a valuable employee, and I'll be sorry to see you go one day, but I realize that by helping you achieve your true goal in life, you will be happier. And happy people make great employees.' With cheerfulness and contentment, she'll give you 100 percent and earnestly train someone to replace herself when she moves on to her new career."

Mr. Cams continues, "Just imagine Nancy's excitement when, a few days later, you show a genuine interest in her goal by giving her a variety of brochures from local nursing academies—brochures you requested on her behalf. You then tell her she can take a few minutes each day on the company phone to contact the schools and set up a class schedule that works for her.

"Now, here's where the true mentoring comes in. You take a moment to share with her your experiences with change. You reflect on how you felt and the fears you faced when you gave up your job to start at the company she works for now. You detail how you overcame obstacles and shut out the noise of the naysayers who told you all the reasons your idea was crazy and why you should forget about it. You let her know you're there to act as a positive support, a constant reminder that she can achieve her dream. You reinforce the message that if and when she needs guidance, encouragement, or a shoulder to lean on during her transition, she can count on you.

"Consider how great Nancy will feel walking into the office each day knowing that, at the end of regular business hours, she'll be heading right toward her life's goal—to become a nurse and help others. How will she answer your company phone from that day forward? What do you suppose her tone of voice and enthusiasm level will be when someone asks her about the place where she works?"

"Wow," says John, "I can just imagine what a terrific first impression she'll make on potential customers and job applicants who walk through the front door every day!"

"It paints a really pretty picture, doesn't it?" questions the mentor.

"It sure does," replies the eager student.

"Mentoring your way to millions is a win-win proposition," Mr. Cams continues. "Let's face it, the more you help others identify and pursue their dreams, the greater support and backing you get from them in return. It just makes sense! No one wants to be just a cog in the system, a faceless wage slave, day in and day out for the rest of their lives.

"When you show your people that you recognize their worth, and you support not only their goals in the workplace but their hopes and dreams outside the system, they'll do amazing things. They'll rise above adversity and give their all to you and your business. Why? Because you've given them something all too rare in life—unconditional support. After all, they're family.

"Step back and imagine, if you will, your company filled with people who feel important and appreciated. People who actually want to come to work each day. What if your job became making the rounds and checking that everyone was keeping up with their life goals as well as their job assignments? Guess what? It can happen!

"Just look up there," Mr. Cams suggests as he points to another banner on the wall. It reads:

The Greatest Success
We'll Know
Is Helping Others
Succeed and Grow

LIKE A LIGHT BULB GOING ON, John abruptly shouts, "By George, I think I've got it!" and the two men stride purposefully out of the factory and burst through another set of gigantic doors.

Chapter 5

A Positive Attitude Gets Results

"WHAT'S DOWN HERE?" the apprentice asks as the two men head down the hallway together.

"The past, the present, and the future," responds the mentor.

"Okay, Charles Dickens. Is this the part where you start reciting lines from A Christmas Carol?" jokes John.

Mr. Cams lets out a belly laugh and says, "You'd think so, with a setup like that, but I'm just going to take you into our Wall of Fame room. At least your mind-set is in keeping with our movie theme, isn't it?"

John is curious and asks, "Hey, speaking of the movie theme, what made you choose that as your decorating style?"

"Well, among other things, as you know, our company supplies movie projectors, posters, and wall decorations for movie houses—just like we did for your grandfather years back. And since we've become successful by taking action while chasing a dream, we put it all together and get 'Lights, Camera, Action!' The decorating theme seemed obvious. Considering the fact that we sell this great stuff, we might as well use it ourselves too. Right?"

The two come to a doorway adorned with similar red velvet theater curtains as those John noticed on his mentor's office window during their first meeting.

"Ta-da," says Mr. Cams as they enter the room.

John is flabbergasted. A gallery of photos wallpapers the entire room.

"This is what we call our Wall of Fame," explains Mr. Cams. "As you can see, however, it's really grown into our room of fame because we've almost run out of empty wall space.

"This wall shows the way the company looked under my father's care, and this wall shows what it looked like before him. This area shows all the family members under my regime, and the empty little spot in this corner is saved for the next group after me."

"This is great," exclaims John. "How do you keep coming up with this stuff?"

"Again, I'd like to take the credit, but it was my mother who collected all the photos. After someone came up with the whole Wall of Fame idea, I started tacking up the pictures so everyone could see where we came from and where we're going."

"What's this?" John asks as he points to a diagram posted on a section of the wall.

"It's the future," answers Mr. Cams, "the bigger picture. It's what we believe is the company's destiny. The missus and I will probably just be spectators through that transition, watching someone else's passion catch fire. We've had a great run here. It's best to know when enough is enough, though, and simply let the new generation take over, as my father did before me, and his before him, and so on. But let's go. There's something else I want to show you."

The two head out of the room, in identical strides. Young John now mirroring Mr. Cams's quick pace to perfection.

Nearing the main office where they'd met the day before, they turn a corner. Before the mentor can even speak, John reads the banner hanging on the wall:

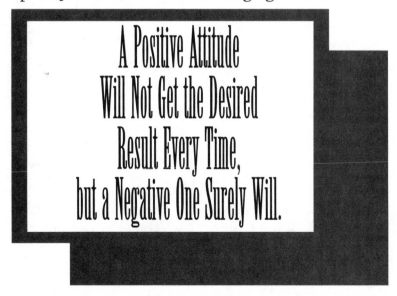

A Positive Attitude
Will Not Get the Desired
Result Every Time,
but a Negative One Surely Will.

"GREAT QUOTE. Who said it?"

"My good friend Anon did," answers the mentor.

"Anon?" John asks.

"Yes, you may know him yourself. Anon Ymous," Mr. Cams winks at his pupil. "I'm sure some great philosopher said it first, but I don't know who to give the credit to."

John actually laughs and thinks to himself, This guy knows how to smile about anything.

"I'll tell you a quick story about this message," begins Mr. Cams, when suddenly Ellen Cams appears out of nowhere and cheerfully interjects, "No, let me tell it. This poor boy is probably tired of hearing you ramble on all day."

"Well, actually . . ." the lad denies.

"Hush up, now," insists Mrs. Cams. "It's my turn to talk."

The two gentlemen exchange a grin and an It looks like she told us look as Ellen begins to speak.

"You see, my husband is an avid tennis player. Not a great one, but an avid one," she says winking at Mr. Cams. "Well, someone made a comment to him on the tennis court one time that really got him thinking. The person was a much more talented player and he was beating Oscar to a pulp. Oscar piped up in his usual manner, 'Here I come. Watch out now; here comes my 'A' game. I have you right where I want you. I hear the theme from Rocky in the background.'"

Mr. Cams chimes in, "No big deal—just the usual pep talk, right? The funny thing is that I actually believed I could pull out a win if I just kept focusing on enjoying the game and played my best. However, it was how my opponent responded that really got me thinking. He said, 'You know, it's great that you have such a positive attitude and everything, but that's not going to win you games.'

"Wow, what a statement, I thought to myself, and rushed right home afterward to write down a thought that I eventually made into this banner: A positive attitude will not get the desired result every time; however, a negative one surely will."

"Mr. Cams did win that tennis match, by the way," says Mrs. Cams with a smile. She continues the dialogue as if she and her husband have rehearsed this routine. "You see, every successful individual we know, past or present, has one true common variable we can think of: Successful people all have an overly zealous positive attitude and clearly believe they will ultimately succeed. Think of all the great American icons who shared the same characteristics. Imagine such people as Henry Ford, Steve Jobs, and the Wright brothers."

John adds, "Thomas Edison, Bill Gates, and

Abraham Lincoln."

"Yes!" Mrs. Cams congratulates. "Can you imagine any of them saying something like, 'This is too hard, I'm way out of my league, or let's just forget about it'?"

Mr. Cams booms in, "Of course not! They kept pushing on through all their adversities and setbacks, believing they'd eventually succeed as long as they kept believing in the beauty of their dream."

"It reminds me of what my old coach used to tell me," says John. "Quitters never win, and winners never quit."

"So, now I put this same scenario to you," Mr. Cams says in a game-show-host tone. "What would you do, right now, if you believed that you, too, couldn't fail? Would you ask that person you've had a crush on out on a date? What about taking action on that crazy idea or invention that you've simply been putting off until the right time? Would you write a book? Adopt a child? Start a new business? Challenge a better player in tennis? What?" Mr. Cams excitedly asks, his arms flapping in the air.

Mrs. Cams calms the moment. "When you think about it, we all have wonderful things running through our minds from time to time. We get all excited about an idea, but then what happens? We let stinkin' thinkin' set in—that's what! We talk ourselves into believing it's never going to work, the challenge is too great, or that special someone won't like us because of the car we drive. What if they say no? What if our idea doesn't work? What if no one reads our book? In other words—"

"We give ourselves reasons to fail," John jumps in.

"Or even worse—reasons to never take a chance or put our dreams into action in the first place," says Mrs. Cams, finishing the thought in tag-team fashion.

Mr. Cams keeps going as soon as Ellen pauses to take a breath. "Here's a big newsflash," he says. "Assuming we don't already have a special someone, a book, or an idea in motion, what do we have to lose? However, by taking the first step of believing in ourselves, our dreams, and our desires, while maintaining a positive attitude toward the outcome, we can only move in one direction."

"Forward!" John keeps the conversation going with an example of his own. "It reminds me of a friend of mine. A week or so ago, we were having lunch together at a restaurant. We spotted this beautiful woman there, and my friend said how much he'd love to go out with her. I suggested that he go over to her and ask her out on a date, but he replied, 'What if she says no?' I said, 'She's already not going out with you, so you have nothing to lose here. In reality, you can only gain a date.'"

"So, no matter what, he can't fail," says Mr. Cams. "The worst thing that can happen is your friend does- n't go out with her. Like you said, he's already doing that!"

"Right!" John responds. "I really like this one. It makes sense and gets me to thinking."

"If you like that, let's finish our day by going by my office. I'll show you something that changed my life," offers the older gentleman.

Realizing that an irresistible offer has just present- ed itself, John agrees. Bidding a temporary farewell to Mrs. Cams, the two companions head toward the big oak doors leading back to the main entrance.

Chapter 6

It Doesn't Matter Who Gets the Credit

A S THE TWO GENTLEMEN reenter the host's unique office, John speaks first. "Wait a second," he says with a grin. "Where's the banner for this lesson?"

"There is no banner for this one, dear boy," the mentor replies.

The young entrepreneur melodramatically acts as though he's going to shed a tear, until Mr. Cams reveals, "But I do have a plaque." Pointing to a wooden carving on his desk, he says, "I saw this years ago on Ronald Reagan's desk in the Oval Office, and it changed my view of things—especially business—in a wonderful way."

Young John reads it aloud:

"THERE IS NO LIMIT TO WHAT A MAN CAN DO SO LONG AS HE DOES NOT CARE A STRAW WHO GETS THE CREDIT FOR IT."
—CHARLES EDWARD MONTAGUE

MR. CAMS CONTINUES, "Do you remember, John, when you first came into my office, and I told you that I was a lot like you in my past?"

The pupil nods yes.

"Well, here's what I meant by that. You see, you came barging into this building with so much arrogance that it would be intimidating to most, yet with an enthusiasm that keeps people around. Everyone wants to back a winning team, young man, but few will stay after the victory if they're not appreciated for their contributions."

John's head slumps onto his chest for only a moment, then rises to meet Mr. Cams's eyes as he says in a humbled tone, "I get it. All this time I was bragging about my own accomplishments, telling everyone how great I was in creating success in my life when, after all, it was those around me who actually did the work. I just took the credit for it."

"Excellent!" applauds Mr. Cams.

"It is?" replies a startled John Bishop.

"Yes. Of all the things you've learned, this is the most important: We are only as good as the company we keep."

John nods a look of understanding and says, "So, it's like you said before—to be truly successful, surround yourself with only the best people you can find, treat them like family, help them attain their goals through mentorship, and let them share in the success."

"Sounds pretty nice, doesn't it?" asks a voice from behind him.

Turning around quickly, John sees a much older man in a wheelchair positioned at the door.

"You must be Mr. Bishop, the chosen one I've been hearing so much about. Let me introduce myself. My name is Mr. Cams—senior, that is. The same message that you just recited, I learned from my father, then shared with the young whippersnapper before you here, my son, Cams Jr."

John turns and looks at his host with a warm smile wrapped in an expression of disbelief at the thought of his mentor still being child in someone's eyes. "I'm sorry," John says uncertainly, returning his attention to the man in the doorway. "Did you say the chosen one?"

"Sure did. You don't think you're standing here for nothing, do you? Listen, I know you've had a long day, so this will be the final story a Cams will share with you today. Let me assure you right now that, yes, you are the chosen one. In fact, we are all the chosen ones.

"Think about it. Right now, I'm sure there's something you're an expert in, something you have a true passion toward, perhaps a sport you play, the company you run, your community involvement, or simply finding great fulfillment in the family you hold together. When all is said and done, haven't we all pondered the age-old question: What is the meaning of life? Well, perhaps it's not so much the meaning of life itself that's so puzzling, but the more personal questions of: What's my purpose? and What's the meaning of my life?

"I believe we were all put on Earth for a purpose, young man, and it's our job to find out what that purpose is. Then, even more important, we need to fulfill that calling by taking action on it."

As the wise old man stops to gather his thoughts, Cams Jr. continues, "Have you ever wondered how and why Greenpeace activists throw themselves in front of freightliners? Or why firefighters rush into places others are escaping? Or why some executives or inventors spend their whole lives in pursuit of what drives them? This is their passion. This is their purpose. And in pursuing that passion, these people are separated from the masses by just one thing—they're living the life they love."

"Wow," exclaims John. "Perhaps the reason I've hit the glass ceiling, as I told you when we first met, is because I've always looked at my business as a business, rather than as something I live to do."

"Do you want to know the secret to ultimate fulfillment?" asks Mr. Cams Sr.

"Of course," replies the eager student.

"Find out what that purpose is for you, and then pursue it with everything you have. Then you'll never be worried about what positions people hold in your company, or that you may have to take one step back to go twenty steps forward. All those things won't matter, because each day you'll be living the life you love, the life you've chosen, rather than one that has chosen you."

"And that's why you don't worry about switching positions here, or who gets the credit, or even if they wish to do something else one day, because you're focused on what you love," John discovers.

As John finishes voicing his revelation, an idea hits him from out of nowhere, and he says to his new friends, "Thank you so much for your time today. Words cannot express how much I appreciate your help."

"You're right," firmly agrees Mr. Cams Sr. "Words cannot express it. Show us how much you appreciate the advice by actually applying it."

The young man stops in his tracks and says, "Yes Sir, I will."

Mr. Cams Sr. continues, "Let me end our conversation here by sharing this last thought with you before you leave. One of the greatest secrets to truly living a balanced and fruitful life is to remember to practice what you preach, because someone is always watching."

"They are?" asks John.

"Yes, they are. Remember, in some form, in some way, to somebody, while you're on this big spinning rock we call Earth, whether you signed up for it or not, no matter how large or small, you're going to make an impact on someone else's life. We all have a special gift to share with the world. We all are the chosen ones, so we owe it to ourselves and everyone to find out what our special gift is and make an impact by pursuing it."

"And since this is true," interrupts the younger Cams, finishing his father's message, "the impact we make should be a positive one. In other words, shouldn't we all do our very best to make a positive impact?"

John acknowledges the two wise gentlemen by nodding his humbled head in agreement and whispers, "Absolutely," like he's just been given the secrets of the universe.

As he prepares to leave, John reaches out to shake their hands, but Mr. Cams Jr. walks over and sends him off with one of his usual bear hugs. John's face lights up. He hugs both Camses back and waves good-bye as he steps out the door and heads for home.

Chapter 7

Wake Up & Live the Life You Love

In the parking structure, John arrives at his bright red Ferrari, sitting where he'd left it such a short time ago. Glancing at the rear window, he reads a sticker that says, "HE WHO DIES WITH THE MOST TOYS WINS."

Suddenly realizing how foolish he's been, John reaches into his pocket for his Platinum Visa card and uses it to feverishly scrape under the decal, trying to remove it as quickly as he can.

There's an old saying that goes: Many receive good advice but few actually profit from it. John is the exception to this rule. One talent he possesses makes him shine above the rest. For you see, John was smart enough to make the appointment to meet his new mentor to begin with, and then, even more important, he's smart enough to realize he needs to follow the great advice he's just been given.

As John gets into his car and starts the engine, he chuckles to himself once more, realizing how childish his behavior has been. He's been arrogant, with an inflated, self-righteous attitude, believing the world owed him everything while he owed little in return. He feels like a giant mirror has been placed before him, and he finally knows how others have been seeing him for a long time. This sudden "reflection" reminds him of a quote in a movie he once saw: We all need mirrors to remind us of who we are.

The next morning, John enters his company as he's done for years—only this time he notices some differences. Or perhaps they aren't really differences as much as he's finally seeing them for the first time.

As the receptionist behind the front desk tries to juggle all the phone calls that appear to be overwhelming her at the moment, he notices a panicked look on her face as though all she wishes for is one moment of peace to take a breath.

Entering the elevator, John notices three coworkers on board. As they all rise together to the floor on which they work, John, for the first time, becomes aware that none of them have spoken to him or even acknowledged that he's there. They all just stare up at the flashing numbers as the floors pass by.

Reaching the grand entrance to his office, he notices that the doors are closed. As he draws near, his assistant simply says, "Your messages, sir." At this moment, John realizes she's been with him for over three years and he doesn't know anything about her—where she lives, or even the names of her children, whose photos are on display all around her desk.

As John opens the doors to his workspace, he's hit in the face with a blast of musky odor emitting from his dark, overcrowded office. He notices for the first time that the windows haven't been opened in years, and the blinds have been drawn shut to keep out the sunshine.

In his huge corner office with the big windows that no one can look out of, John sits behind his over-sized, solid mahogany desk with the huge nameplate to match, raised on a perch (so he sits higher than anyone seated in the chair across from him). Still holding his car keys in his hand, he glances at the Ferrari symbol and unhappily begins to think to himself, reflecting on the comment made to Mr. Cams about A Christmas Carol. People must believe I'm totally self-centered, greedy, and maybe even mean. They probably envision me as another Ebenezer Scrooge.

Looking around his workspace, he realizes there are no color photos of his family or things he loves in his life—only charts, memos, and Post-it notes to remind him of his next deadline. The only exception is a faded black-and-white picture tucked in the corner of the room. It shows John and his father standing in front of his granddad's old theater, back when it was the pride of the town.

How did I even make it this far? John wonders to himself, shaking his head in self-disappointment as he lowers his forehead onto his palms.

> ### At this moment, the change begins.

"COME IN HERE FOR A MOMENT, won't you Mary?" John calls out to his trusted assistant.

As she walks into the room, he asks her to hand over the pencil and notepad she has in tow.

"We won't need these today," says John.

The look of shock on Mary's face speaks volumes. She's not quite sure if John is feeling ill or if he's drunk. He's never begun his day without boisterously dictating his schedule to the help.

"What may I do for you?" asks Mary as she takes her customary seat across from her supervisor.

"The first thing you can do for me," begins the new Mr. Bishop, "is to help me brighten this place up a bit. Let's open these blinds and windows, for gosh sakes, and let the light in. Please order some plants for this office. And, even more important, order some flowers for your desk."

Again, Mary's look is one of disbelief and amazement.

John then asks her to go to the local success store and purchase some motivational banners and posters to place around the office.

What comes next is a surprise to both of them. John says, "Before you do that, would you please do me a personal favor? I know it's not your job, but would you please go downstairs and help the receptionist answer the phones? It seems she's overwhelmed and could use some assistance right now. In fact, if that's the case, kindly let me know so we can be sure to get her some permanent help right away."

Mary's face lights up at the proposition. "I'd be very happy to, Sir," she replies.

"Sir, nothing," continues John. "From now on, please call me J.B.

"You must be wondering what's come over me, and I'll explain later. What's important for you to know right now is that I've met someone who's helping me become a new person, and I'd appreciate your help in developing a new environment. I want everyone to be happy to work here and proud to be part of this company."

"I'd be delighted to help you, Sir—I mean J.B.," Mary replies with a wink.

After opening the windows and blinds and spraying some fragrance, Mary leaves the office and begins her assignment of making it a more people-friendly place. As the breeze blows through John's sunlit office for the first time, it seems as if the wind has uplifted him and given him a breath of fresh air—in more ways than one.

Days go by, which turn into months, and eventually, five years. A little bit older and a lot wiser, John still meets with his mentor on a regular basis, and now he mentors others as well. Though he experiences great success, he still feels something is missing. His company has made a complete turnaround, yet he still feels a little empty inside.

On his fortieth birthday, John realizes what's been missing. That morning, he has an appointment for a relaxing massage from Janine, the newest employee at his usual spa. During his rubdown, he speaks with her, asking, "How many hours a day do you work here?"

"Not a single one," she replies.

John jerks his head abruptly and asks, "What do you mean? You're working now."

"Hardly," she offers in the softest of tones. "I love what I do, so it's not work to me. Someone once asked me, when I was young, what I would do for a living if I did it for free. After many jobs and much thought, this is the living I chose. It's the perfect career for me, and it keeps me balanced."

"Balanced, you say?" John inquires with sincere interest.

"Yes. I've found that the secret to happiness is having all the parts of your life in order—physical, spiritual, emotional, mental, and of course, financial."

"Well, that's pretty deep. I'm going to have to think on that for a bit," says John.

The kind woman offers, "You do that, but for now just relax."

The birthday boy enjoys the rest of his therapy. When they're through, he sits up and asks Janine one last question, "Why do you like massage therapy so much? I mean, what do you get out of it?"

"Massage is only part of my personal secret to happiness. I've traveled the world, and I've decided that my passion lies in business, which is what really brings me here."

John glances at her with an odd look because her answer doesn't add up to him.

"Let me explain," she continues. "Over the past eleven years, I've been managing spas all over the world, from Bombay to Jamaica. I've learned everything about operating spas—from saunas to exercise rooms to mineral pools to marketing the business. I've decided I want to open a spa of my own one day soon."

"That's great," John says enthusiastically, "but it still doesn't explain why you're here, working on me now."

"Well, the only part missing from my complete knowledge of the industry was doing the massages myself, so I signed up for classes and now I'm putting into practice what I've learned. The final step for me now is to open my own location. This way, I can relate to everyone who works with me, and I can fill any position if need be. It makes plenty of sense to me."

John's jaw almost hits the floor as he realizes the similarities between what she's saying and what his mentor talked about so many lessons before.

Leaving the club that day, John has a renewed zest to his step that he hasn't felt in years. The next day, he shows up at the office in his new usual manner, waves at the first-floor receptionist, Rhonda (who now has her own assistant), and gets into the elevator where he chats warmly with everyone on board. As he walks through the brightly painted hallway into his office, he glances up to see the first banner he placed on his wall—the message taught to him by his mentor. It reads: Make a Positive Impact.

He stops to speak with his assistant, Mary, to see how her weekend went and how her oldest son did in his ballgame the night before. When they finish catching up, John walks into his office. As he takes his seat behind his smaller, more functional desk decorated with photos of his family and friends, he calls out, "Mary, would you please come in here? I would like to discuss something with you."

"What's up, J.B.?" Mary asks as she strolls into his office and takes a seat.

"I'm giving a month's notice today that I'm leaving the firm, and I wanted you to be the first to know. It's time I followed my passion, as everyone keeps saying, and I'm ready to take a chance to pursue what I love."

"That's wonderful, John," she says with a smile. "What are you going to pursue?"

"Right there," he says with pride in his voice as he points to a neatly framed picture. It's the same as the one that had been tucked away before, showing him and his father in front of the old movie house. Only now it's been blown up and color has been added to the black and white image.

"I always hoped to follow in my grandfather's footsteps, and now that I have the ability and have found the true desire to do so, I believe I will. Here's one of the best parts—I'm recommending to the board that you take over my position. You've learned everything I do here and, to be honest, you've done most of the work for me over these past few years. It's only fair that you get recognized for all you've accomplished for this company."

Mary is astonished. She stands up, walks around the desk, hugs John, and says, "Thank you so much, J.B. I'm deeply touched by your faith in me."

Our young Mr. Bishop leaves his position four weeks later, and even though he feels some jitters inside about facing his next great quest, he knows it will all be worth it. He's about to do something most people only dream of: Wake up and live the life you love!

John's new business goes better than he'd hoped. His grandfather would have been so proud. The theater becomes the talk of the town once more, reopening as a state-of-the-art facility that everyone wants to attend.

John has never felt better. He's pursuing his ultimate dream, coincidentally in an industry needed by his greatest ally, Oscar Cams. The two of them form a business relationship that creates more abundance in each of their lives than they ever could have imagined. They work fantastically together, opening new theaters all over the state and creating one of the largest chains that has ever graced the land.

They do so well that, during an interview for a local newspaper, when a reporter asks the secret to his success, John replies, "Most people in business think—what's the least I can pay to get someone to work for me? Now, thanks to some great wisdom bestowed unto me, my new attitude is: What's the most you can afford to share to get someone to work with you?

"I only surround myself with the very best people—the Tiger Woodses of accounting, the Bill Gateses of sales and marketing, and the Oprah Winfreys of human resources. Then, since I've hired only the best, I allow them to do their jobs, treat them like they're part of my family, and share the profits with them.

"And you know what? I don't even have to manage them because they're the best in their field, and they manage their departments and themselves. In return for this relationship, they treat the company as if it were their own. And it is. It really belongs to all of us—we're all involved in its success."

Fascinated, the reporter asks if John faced tough times getting started.

"Of course I did," John replies. "That's part of life. However, since I was so focused on the end result and not so caught up in the little things that happened along the way, I never got caught up in the moguls."

"The moguls?" asks the reporter

"Yes, the moguls. Imagine that I'm standing in my skis atop a mountain, getting ready to race to the bottom. I'm focused on getting to the finish line. Now, along the way, there are moguls, trees, black ice, and bitter cold weather. You know—obstacles! But since I know they're coming, they don't really bother me. Other people get caught up in them. They fall down, get up, and fall down again. Unfortunately, at this point—cold, wet, and maybe hurt—most stay down. Yet when I fall down, no matter how many times, I don't let it affect my attitude, stop my forward progress, or—most important— make me lose my focus on the end result."

"Getting to the fireplace in the ski lodge," the reporter chimes in.

"You got it," John says with a laugh.

"Let me ask you," continues the reporter. "How did you make your first million?"

"As strange as it is, I did it by not chasing millions. I did it by finding something I was passionate about and then pursued it with everything I had. In the book, The Millionaire Mentor, you'll find one of my favorite quotes: When you do what you love and love what you do, you'll have success your whole life through. That's why I tell everyone I mentor to find their passion and then money will follow—like it did for Ted Turner, Bill Cosby, Donald Trump, and others. These people focused on their passion, and the money chased after them."

"Why do you say there's no such thing as a slacker?" the reporter continues to probe.

"Well, simple really. If you lined up everyone in a row and asked if they wanted to be financially independent, not too many would pipe up and say they'd rather live in a box under a bridge, right?

"I think of it this way. Think of the laziest oaf you know, that guy who never gets off the sofa except to get more chips. You know who I mean. Then imagine walking into the room and asking if he wants to go to the big game with you. What would happen? He'd jump up, shower, put on his favorite gear, and off to the stadium you'd go!

"Well, there are hundreds of people who literally get to do just that every day—the sportscasters, the refs, even the towel boys are doing something that most can only dream about. They're actually loving and living the life they choose. They're passionate about their work, so like I said before, they're really never working at all."

"Why should a person start his or her own business? Isn't starting your own business a very risky thing to do?" the reporter asks.

"Let me ask you a question. Didn't the people you

work for now at some time start their own business—where you now find yourself working for
them as a job? Or what I like to call a J.O.B.—and we
all know what that sands for—Just Over Broke! The
only difference between you and them is that they
put their fears aside and took action. Now, what's
stopping you?"

When the article appears in the local newspaper,
the whole town comes to know the real John Bishop.

Chapter 8

Welcome to the Family!

DAYS, MONTHS, AND MORE YEARS pass by, as does our friend, Mr. Cams Sr. Though he is deeply missed, the tears shed on his behalf are happy ones in celebration of the rich, full life of an endearing man who touched the hearts of many.

John stays in touch with the aging Oscar and Ellen Cams and becomes like a son to them—a true blessing, as they never had children of their own. They spend holidays together and help one another's companies and charities become the best they can be.

When John left Mr. Cams's office, so many years ago now, he decided to turn things around for both himself and others. Five years later, he became the talk of the town—this time because of the wonderful things he did for the community while creating his own corporation around his ultimate passion.

Today, his business is better than ever, and the relationships he developed have become legendary throughout his city. Everyone wants to meet this man so they, too, can learn the secrets to his success.

Arriving at his mentor's office for a visit, John is greeted by the same receptionist he met on that very first day. "Mr. Cams will see you now," Ellen says in a mock-professional manner.

"Nonsense," John says as he rounds the desk to give her a warm and gentle hug.

"My, how you've changed since we first met, John Bishop. Now, you go in there," Ellen directs as she points to the door and pats him on the back.

John enters the room to see Oscar staring out his big window, with an ease to his expression John hasn't witnessed before.

"What's the story, morning glory?" asks John in singsong fashion.

"It's time we had a little talk," begins the mentor. "Walk with me."

John, hearing the seriousness in his friend's tone, gives him a look of concern as the two walk out the door and down the familiar hallway.

"Go inside," Oscar directs as he holds back the curtain to the Wall of Fame room they first visited together so long ago.

As John takes his first step into the room, he notices a space on the wall now has his picture on it. He looks dazed. "What's going on?" he murmurs.

"Congratulations," says Ellen, who has walked in quietly to stand beside her husband. She places her arm around John's shoulders and says, "We want you to have this."

"Have what?" John asks.

Oscar looks proudly at John and says, "You've become more than a friend to us over the years. Your actions have proven more about your character than anyone could ever describe. You walked through our doors a different person from the person you are today. Now that it's time for us to retire and move on, we want to offer you our corporation. Combined with your company that is already in place, you'll be an unstoppable force. But more important, we believe in our hearts that you'll know what to do with such power."

John stands there stunned, feeling the same deer-in-the-headlights sensation he felt so many years before. After a moment or two of silence, he says, "It will be my honor, my privilege, and my promise to live up to the expectations and dreams you've worked so diligently to create. The first thing I'd like to do as the new CEO is request that the two of you join me and head up our advisory board, to oversee the transition and continue to be part of something that tremendously affects the lives of so many family members."

"We accept," Ellen agrees without asking her husband. "Now, let's go celebrate!"

As the three good friends, smiling broadly, walk out of the Wall of Fame room into the factory, a new banner adorns the rafters. As John steps into his future, he reads . . .

Universal Success Secrets

•

Always maintain a positive,
solution-searching attitude.

•

To truly succeed at anything, our chances
increase when we enjoy the task—for
when we do what we love, and love what
we do, we'll have success our
whole life through.

•

The only limitations we really have are
those we give ourselves.

•

The only expectations we need fulfill
are those we give ourselves.

•

There is nothing as powerful as a positive
attitude, and nothing as detrimental as a
negative one.

•

●

Morally speaking, if we have to wonder whether something is right or wrong, chances are, it's wrong.

●

When we focus on other people's success, ours is sure to follow.

●

Live your word—lead by example.

●

Share. (Wealth + Information + Glory = Success)

●

The best chance of reaching a goal is to simply give yourself one to reach.

●

Observe every obstacle as a learning experience. The greater the challenge, the greater the reward.

●

•

Do the hardest thing first—the rest will be easy.

•

Treat others the way THEY want to be treated.

•

Few great accomplishments have ever been achieved alone; seek support from those with talents that exceed your own.

•

We are the reflection of the five people we associate with the most, and our income is the average of those five people. Choose your friends wisely.

•

A dream written down with a date becomes a GOAL. A goal broken down into steps becomes a PLAN. A plan backed by ACTION, makes your dream come true.

•

•

We learn more about someone's character on one bad day, than on all their good days put together. The true measure of all great leaders is how well they weather storms.

•

It's better to invest time doing what pleases you, rather than to waste time trying to please everyone else.

•

In the end, the extent of our own success will be measured by the accomplishments that we have helped create in others.

•

Having potential simply means that you possess talents and abilities that you are not applying.

•

Things are the way you think they are, because you think they are that way. Our perception determines our experience.

Notes

Notes

Notes

Notes

Notes

Notes